Dani and His Amazing Paintbrush
Dani's Daring Daydream

Illustrated by Nathalia Milagros Rivera Pérez
Written by Dr. Daniela Fifi

Author website: drdanielafifi.com

Published by Victory Education
ISBN: 9798990663510

This book is dedicated to the Trinidadian artist **Geoffrey Holder**. It was inspired by his mural painting at the Hilton Hotel in Trinidad and Tobago. Geoffrey Holder was an actor, dancer, visual artist, and musician. He was inspired by many different cultures around the world and was particularly drawn to art and artists from the Caribbean. He admired its mixture of people and the bright colors of its landscape. At that time in history, the fashion, dance, and musical styles of the Caribbean were seen as very bold. A striking figure in the art world, Geoffrey was proud to represent his home country.

Dani loves to do all sorts of different things. He loves drawing, playing, acting, singing, wiggling, jiggling, and dancing! But most of all, Dani loves to paint. With his amazing paintbrush, he can create almost anything!

Dani likes crazy shapes and super bright colors. He tries to wear as many as possible!

At home, he makes clothes from all kinds of materials. Dad often helps him paint T-shirts and jackets to make them more fun and exciting. Dani loves his funky shoes and fantastic hats.

One day, Dani wears his favorite shoes to school. Sitting at his desk, he cannot wiggle, jiggle, or dance. Instead, he does the next best thing. Dani stares out of the window and begins to daydream...

Suddenly, the daydream ends because Dani's classmates are laughing!

"Why are you wearing those shoes?" asks one kid. "They're weird!" says another.

Dani doesn't know what to say. All of a sudden, he feels sad.

Luckily, his best friend Boscoe comes to the rescue. "Leave Dani alone!" says Boscoe. "It's not nice to tease someone because they are different."

Boscoe is a lot like Dani. He enjoys dancing, dressing up, and playing music—especially on steel-pan drums!

"Come over to my house," says Boscoe. "I know just how to cheer you up."

That night, Dani and Boscoe play drums for hours. They play until it gets dark!

"Thanks," says Dani. "Music always makes me feel better."

The next day at school, Dani doesn't wear any bright colors. He worries that the kids will tease him again.

Today, Dani's favorite teacher, Mr. Samedi, teaches theater class. Like Dani, Mr. Samedi loves wiggling, jiggling, and dancing. He loves to be creative more than anything!

"I'd like you to create a performance," says Mr. Samedi. "You could dance, paint, tell a story... or even play the flute! The most important thing is to be bold and creative. The more different and creative you are, the better."

Dani teams up with Boscoe. Before long, he goes from feeling excited to sad. When the bell rings, Mr. Samedi asks him to stay behind.

"What's wrong, Dani?" asks Mr. Samedi.

Dani sighs, "I'm not sure I want to be different."

Mr. Samedi smiles kindly and says, "Dani, you are an artist. I can tell! I saw how boldly you painted your shoes. I know you are a daydreamer like me."

Dani is amazed and asks Mr. Samedi, "You have daydreams, too?"

Mr. Samedi laughs loudly and replies, "Of course. I daydream all the time!" He kneels beside Dani and softly whispers, "I daydream whenever I want to be creative. I follow my daydreams, even if they seem weird to others. You see, Dani, only when we do something different do we discover something new."

"Wow," says Dani. "I never thought of it like that."

Mr. Samedi leaps to his feet and says, "Stay in the theater at lunchtime and let your imagination go. I dare you to be different, Dani. I dare you to see where your daydreams lead you." In the blink of an eye, Mr. Samedi is gone.

Dani shuts his eyes and begins to dream...

When Dani opens his eyes, the world is all white.
He can't see anything!

Just then, a man appears. He has a wide smile, and
he wears a tall top hat. He looks very familiar.

Dani gasps. "Mr. Samedi?!"

The man laughs loudly. "Not quite!" he replies. "My name is Geoffrey. I'm an artist, just like you. I can tell!"

"How?" asks Dani.

Geoffrey taps his head. "You have a big imagination. That is all an artist needs. When you use your imagination, you can create anything you want."

A paintbrush appears in Geoffrey's hand. When he waves it, Dani's daydream changes. He is standing in a park full of tall, green trees. Dani looks closely at the tree trunks. He can see they are made from brushstrokes!

Geoffrey smiles. "This park is in the Caribbean." He gives Dani the brush. "Now it's your turn to paint."

"Hey!" says Dani. "This is my paintbrush! How did you get it?"

Geoffrey winks. "I used my imagination."

Following his heart, Dani begins to paint. First, he adds a bright sun. It shines through the trees in bright colors. Then he imagines the most fantastic flowers and plants. They are like nothing anyone has ever seen!

Next, Dani paints people walking through the park. The ladies wear long dresses and carry old-fashioned parasols.

He also imagines a grown-up Boscoe wearing a shiny top hat and coat.

He creates the most amazing patterns for the clothes, each garment more colorful than the last one. Every single pattern is different!

Lastly, Dani paints children playing together and a dog running behind them.

A flute appears in Geoffrey's hand. As he plays a tune, the park comes to life!

"What's happening?" asks Dani.

"You dared to be different," says Geoffrey. "When you choose to be bold, the people who see you will follow."

Geoffrey plays his flute, and the people begin to dance. The adults and children join in a circle, clapping and cheering for whoever is dancing in the center. The whole thing is exciting to watch. All of a sudden, Dani's daring daydream ends.

"Dani!" shouts Boscoe's voice. "Lunchtime is over!"

Dani draws a picture of his daydream in class that afternoon. "This is the scene we should perform!" Dani says to Boscoe.

Dani's best friend, Boscoe, looks nervous. "You know I like dressing up," he says. "But this design is so colorful, and the clothes have so many patterns. What if both of us get teased?"

Boscoe points at the other kids working together.

"Everyone else's drawings are neat and tidy, but you've colored outside the lines. This picture is so messy, no one will understand it." Boscoe sighs. "What if your ideas are just too different?"

At that moment, Mr. Samedi passes by.
He winks at Dani.

Dani smiles. "If we choose to be bold, the people who see us will follow."

That night, Dani is very excited. At home, Dad helps
him sew some costumes. Then, Dani picks up his
paintbrush. He paints the clothes in amazing patterns,
as colorful as he can make them.

"These are awesome," says Dad. "Where did you get
your ideas?"

Dani grins. "I used my imagination."

The next day, Dani takes his paintbrush to
school. Boscoe helps Dani turn the theater into
a colorful park! Soon, it is time for their performance.

"I know you're nervous," says Dani. "I'm your friend,
and I am different. Will you do this with me as a team?"

Boscoe looks at the bold costumes and the wild colors
on the wall. Then, he smiles. "You bet," says Boscoe.

The performance begins with Mr. Samedi playing a tune on the flute. When Dani and Boscoe appear on the stage, their classmates gasp at the amazing outfits. The incredible patterns on the performers' clothes seem just as strange as their dancing. Dani and Boscoe wiggle and jiggle, making movements that no one has ever seen! Suddenly, Dani's painting comes to life. Now, the other students are no longer sitting in the audience.

They are standing in the park, surrounded by trees. They are dressed like the people in Dani's daydream! The kids feel the heat of the sun, which shines in bright, beautiful colors. They smell the flowers. They cannot stop themselves from joining in the dance.

"Follow me!" shouts Dani as the students dance in a huge circle.

When the performance ends, Dani's classmates cheer. His paintings have brought color to everyone's life. All the kids agree that being different is a very special thing.

"Thanks, Boscoe," says Dani as they take a bow. "I couldn't have done it without you."

"You're welcome," replies Boscoe. "I can't wait to see what you paint next!"

At the end of the school day,
Mr. Samedi walks with Dani
down the hallway. "So what
have you learned?" he asks.

"I will always dare to be different,"
replies Dani. "I will always dress
brightly, and I will always follow
my heart."

He looks at Mr. Samedi and
thought for a moment. "By the
way, are you related to Geoffrey?"

Mr. Samedi winks.
"Use your imagination."

About the Author

Dr. Daniela Fifi is a doctoral graduate of Art and Art Education from Teachers College, Columbia University in the City of New York. She worked as an art educator in New York City and the Caribbean. She's been awarded several fellowships and awards during her career, including the New York State Assembly - Caribbean Life Impact Award, The Museum Education Research Fellowship at the Whitney Museum of American Art, and the Samuel H. Kress Interpretive Fellowship at The Wallach Art Gallery, Columbia University. She taught art education, world art history, and human development in the arts at The City College of New York and New Jersey City University. She served on the editorial board of the National Art Education Association and also served as the Editor-in-Chief of *Viewfinder: An Art Museum Education E-journal*. Daniela enjoys listening to music and being in nature in her spare time. To learn more about Daniela visit her website: drdanielafifi.com

Special thanks to Vanessa Masters, Narjes Mohammadi, and Benji Kahn.

www.ingramcontent.com/pod-product-compliance
Lightning Source LLC
Chambersburg PA
CBRC102036110726
48005CB00009BA/1040